THE NIGHT BEFORE RAMADAN

Fatima Lhabaz

Illustrated by : Fatmtm Mohamed

"Yes, you are right, my little girl. Grandma and Grandpa are coming to stay with us. As for your question, Omar, I think that your grandparents will want to tell you all about it."

"But Mom, I want to know what Ramadan is right now," moaned Omar.

"Please have some patience, Omar," Mom replied with a smile. "Ramadan begins tomorrow, so your grandparents will be here soon, but the time will pass by more quickly if you help me out in the kitchen."

"Okay. Hurry up, Layla. I'll wash the dishes, and you can set the table."

The table was ready for dinner. The smell of yummy pasta wafted across the house.

"That smells lovely," commented Dad, walking into the kitchen. "I'm getting very hungry now."

"You can't eat yet, Dad," replied Layla. "We have to wait for Grandma and Grandpa."

Just then, the little family heard the honking of a car. "They're here!" cried Omar and Layla as they raced outside.

The shuttlecock flew over Omar's head. "You shouldn't hit the badminton birdie that high, Layla," called out Omar, sneaking his way through a flower bush.

"I'm sorry, Omar. I accidentally hit it too hard," replied Layla.

"Children!" called out Mom. "Guess who's coming to stay with us for Ramadan?"

"Is it Grandma and Grandpa?" asked Layla.

"Awesome!" squealed Omar, skipping. "Wait, what's Ramadan?"

Bismillah (In the name of Allah)

Stories are the best possible way of teaching. Since the beginning of times, we have learned and taught our children through telling stories. Stories bring the lessons alive and make the lessons very easy to adapt. Teaching religion is one of the most difficult concepts to build among young children. But stories make that simple and effective!
We designed this book with the hope of making it easier to introduce your little family members to their faith and grasp the essence of their religion.

"My! Haven't you two grown since the last time I saw you," said Grandpa, smiling.

"My favourite twins! Come here and give Grandma a big hug," Grandma said, reaching out for Omar and Layla.

"Grandma, Grandpa! What's Ramadan?" asked Omar. Grandma and Grandpa laughed.

"Ramadan is a very special time. We'll tell you all about it once we are inside," replied Grandpa.

All through dinner, Omar and Layla waited impatiently to learn about Ramadan.

"Will you tell us about Ramadan now, Grandma?" asked Omar once the table was cleared.

"Ramadan is the ninth month on the Islamic calendar," said Grandma.

"Islamic calendar?" the twins replied, looking at each other in confusion.

"Yes, as Muslims, we follow the Islamic calendar. We also have twelve months: Muharram, Safar, Rabi al-Awwal, Rabi al-Thani, Jumada al-Ula, Jumada al-Thaniyah, Rajab, Shaban, Ramadan, Shawwal, Dhu al-Qadah, and Dhu al-Hijjah," explained Grandpa.

"Throughout Ramadan, Muslims observe something called fasting. Fasting is when we stop eating and drinking for a period of time during the day," Grandma said.

Omar's eyes widened. "How can we stop eating and drinking like that, Grandma?"

"Once you are old enough, you will be able to do it," Grandpa told Omar. "And don't worry! Fasting is only observed from sunrise to sunset. After sunset, it is fine to eat and drink!"

"Do you two know the five daily prayers?" Grandpa asked.

"Yes!" shouted the children.

"What is the first prayer of the day?"

"Fajr," replied Omar.

"Very good. As Muslims, we wake up super early and have a meal before the Fajr Adhan. This meal is called Suhoor. After that, we do not eat or drink anything until the Maghrib Adhan. This meal is called Iftar."

"But why do we stop eating and drinking during Ramadan?" asked Omar.

"Yeah, why, Grandpa?" asked Layla.

"Muslims all over the world fast to show their love for Allah. Fasting teaches us to control ourselves. Even if we are really hungry and want to secretly eat something when we think that no one else is watching, we stop ourselves, because we know that Allah is always watching."

"Yes, and fasting also teaches us what it is like to be hungry, which encourages us to help those who are poor and in need of our help," added Grandma.

"Throughout this month, we also try to do a lot of good deeds that will make Allah happy."

"Like reciting the Quran and praying?" asked Layla.

"Yes, reciting the Quran, praying, giving charity, avoiding unnecessary talk, and being kind to others."

"And that will make Allah very happy!" exclaimed Omar.

"I will fast the whole month," said Omar to Layla.

"Let's take it slowly, my little warrior," Grandma said laughing. "You can start by waking up for Suhoor and fasting for part of the day. When you get hungry, you can eat. Once you are older, you can fast the whole month."

"I won't get hungry, Grandma. I will show you tomorrow."

Omar and Layla woke up early the next morning.
They excitedly ate their Suhoor meal. When
the Adhan was called for Fajr Prayer, the family
stopped eating. Soon, they prayed Fajr, recited the
Quran, and went back to sleep.

When they woke up later that morning, Layla and Omar
were not too hungry. They washed up and went looking
for Grandma and Grandpa. Grandma was doing Dhikr,
while Grandpa was reciting the Quran.

"We are not hungry, Grandma," said Layla proudly.

"That's good. But when you do get hungry, you should eat something," Grandma said, smiling.

All morning long, Omar and Layla helped Mom out in the kitchen as they prepared meals for the poor and the needy. They also made food for their friends and neighbors. They became hungry while working, so Mom gave them some lunch.

During the day, Omar and Layla performed many good deeds that they knew Allah would love. They helped Grandma and Grandpa visit the supermarket to buy canned foods for the poor.

They laid out food and water for the street dogs and cats.

They also visited a homeless shelter and served the people there lunch. It was a very busy day for Omar and Layla.

By the time it was evening, the twins were very tired.
They were sitting around the table discussing their day
when they heard the Maghrib Adhan being called.
Mom, Dad, Grandma, and Grandpa ate one date
each, so Omar and Layla both ate one date each, too.

"It's Sunnah to break your fast with a date fruit," said Dad.

They thanked Allah for the lovely meal.

"I will wake up for Suhoor tomorrow, too," Layla told Dad.

"I will, too," said Omar. "Now, what do we do next?"

"Next, we pray Maghrib. And after Ishaa, we pray a special prayer that is offered only during Ramadan. It's called Taraweeh," said Grandpa.

"Awesome!" cried Layla.

"Ramadan is a lot of fun. I love Ramadan," said Omar.

"I am very pleased to hear that you love Ramadan. But you must remember that whatever good deeds you do during this month should also be continued during the other months of the year. Do you understand, my darlings?" asked Grandma.

"Yes, yes, Grandma! We will continue to do good deeds that Allah loves," replied the twins as they raced to get ready for that night's prayers.

Glossary

Allah   The Arabic word for God

Adhan   The Islamic call to prayer

Suhoor   A meal consumed early in the morning before fasting

Iftar   A meal eaten after sunset to break one's fast during Ramadan

Maghrib   The Arabic word for sunset

Quran   The holy book of Islam

Dhikr   The glorification and remembrance of Allah

Sunnah   The way of Prophet Muhammad (PBUH). It includes everything he said, did, and approved of.

Printed in Great Britain
by Amazon

37325036R00023